Education is Power: A Snippet of The Life of W.E.B. Du Bois

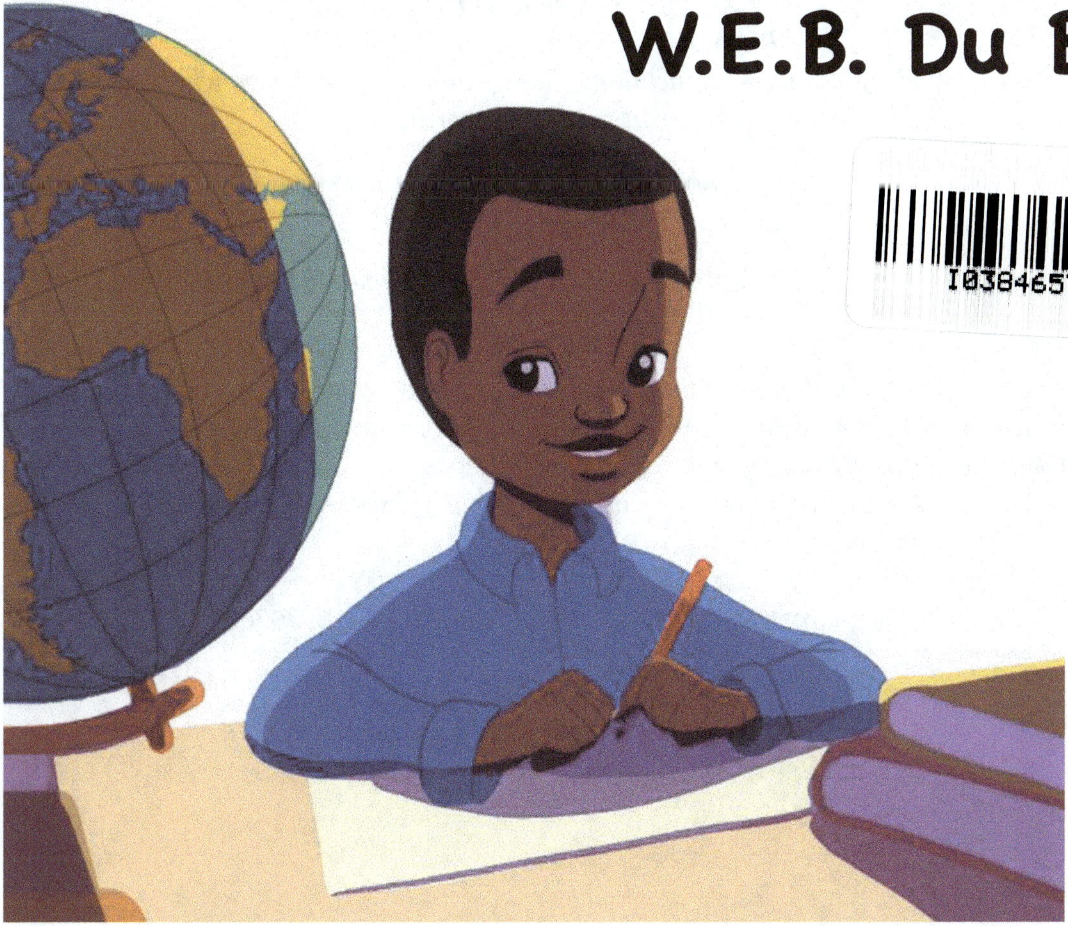

By: Lenny Williams

Published by Melanin Origins LLC
PO Box 122123; Arlington, TX 76012
All rights reserved, including the right of reproduction in whole
or in part in any form.
Copyright 2018

First Edition

The author asserts the moral right under the Copyright, Designs and Patents Act of 1988 to be identified as the author of this work.

All rights reserved. No part of this publication may be reproduced, stored in a retrieval system or transmitted, in any form by any means without the prior consent of the author, nor be otherwise circulated in any form of binding or cover other than that with which it is published and without a similar condition being imposed on the subsequent purchaser.

Library of Congress Control Number: 2018930760

ISBN: 9781626768161 hardback
ISBN: 9781626768123 paperback
ISBN: 9781626768154 ebook

Dedication

I dedicate this book to all of the young dreamers and leaders worldwide. Never give up on your goals, and continue to dream and lead as one. Life will come with obstacles, but I know you all will have the strength to overcome them through faith and through the wisdom that you have obtained over the years.

Lenny Williams

Education is power and it gives us a better understanding of the world around us.

I'm pretty sure your parents and teachers have told you about the amazing things that an education can do for you too!

Hi, my name is W.E.B. Du Bois, and I want to tell you how education changed my life.

She knew that learning new things was very special to me, because I enjoyed studying and earning A's on my tests.

One day she told me if I study really hard, not only would my education give me an honor roll, but it would also give me the ability to do whatever I wanted in life.

Not only is education power, but education gives power to anyone who desires it!

I lived by those words of the adults in my life, and powered my way straight to college.

Actually, I loved learning so much that I went to three different colleges! First, I went to Fisk University and then I attended the University of Berlin.

Fun fact: Did you know that the University of Berlin is in Germany? Education can take you all around the world.

I went on to become the 1st African-American to earn a Doctorate degree from Harvard University, so feel free to call me Dr. Du Bois if you like.

Learning and becoming a great leader was important, but it was also fun! I wanted to share the power of education with my friends so they could join in on the fun too.

So, I created a group known as the Talented Tenth and I helped start the NAACP: the National Association for the Advancement of Colored People.

Creating those groups helped my friends and even complete strangers get an education. As a group of young leaders, we taught them history, math, reading, writing, and science.

I did not stop there either; I continued to share education everywhere I went. I taught a class at Atlanta University in Atlanta, Georgia.

Then I visited the wonderful country of Ghana in West Africa.

I also taught while I was in Ghana, but my favorite part about being in a country far away from home was learning many outstanding things about the many cultures and ways of living that were different from what I was familiar with in America.

No matter where I traveled, one thing remained the same.
Education was always needed.

You have the power to be an astronaut, a doctor, a teacher, or even the owner of your favorite sports team! Anything is possible and there is NO LIMIT!

www.ingramcontent.com/pod-product-compliance
Lightning Source LLC
Chambersburg PA
CBHW081433070526
44586CB00020B/2570